My Name Is Child B

*A standalone story
of one of the 3,500 children
who are murdered by
their caregivers every year*

Jessica Jackson

*Cover Photograph by
Maël Balland of Unsplash
Posed by model*

Copyright Jessica Jackson © 2025 All rights reserved
No part of this book may be reproduced in any form
without written permission from the author
Reviewers may quote brief passages in reviews

*For the purposes of anonymity, names of
siblings and friends have been changed
unless where commonly known*

**This book has details of child abuse
that some readers may find upsetting**

Printed by Amazon
In the unlikely event of errors being made during
the printing process, they will be happy to replace your book

Simply go to Your Orders, Replace
and be sure to write 'faulty' across the cover
before returning your book

Every week in the UK
1-2 children are abused to death
by their parents or caregivers
In the USA, the number
is a staggering 27 children per week

*This is the story
of one of those children*

This work is based on a real case
*The first part of the story is semi-fictionalised,
with some events and dialogue added*

*The second part tells the facts of the case,
detailing the injuries, trials and sentencing*

Contents

Thank You For Choosing This Book 5
Your Free E-book 7
Acknowledgments 8
Introduction 9
My Name is Child B 11
Invitation To My Readers' List 53
Pick Up Your Free Book 54
If You Need A Little Help 55
Enter My Draw 56
Thanks To You 57
The Murder of Jordan Brooks 59
Abuse of Children with Disabilities 75
Help Me To Raise Awareness 81
Your Next Book In The Series 82
Follow me on Amazon 83
Join Us On Facebook 84
Don't Miss A Thing 85
Have You Read All My Books? 86
Prevention 87
Warning Signs of Abuse 88
Selected Resources 91

Thank You For Choosing This Book

If you've made it through the whole series so far, you're amazing.

This child's story is important to me for many reasons, including the fact that these particular voices are seldom heard. So thank you.

> If you can spare a moment when you've finished reading, I'd be very grateful if you'd help to raise awareness of child abuse by rating or reviewing this book.

I hope you will enjoy this 8th Volume in the series, and don't forget your free ebook …

MY NAME IS CHILD B

Your Free E-book
Exclusive only to my readers

The tragic case of Isaiah Torres

(with bonus content about Baby Brianna Lopez)

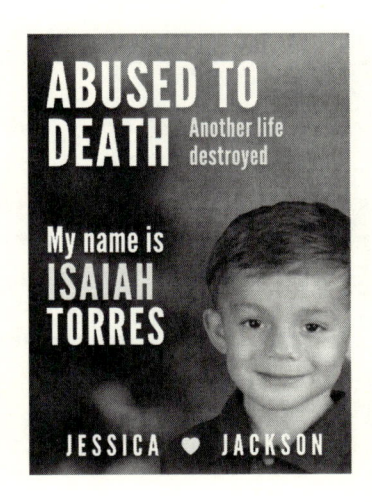

ABUSED TO DEATH — Another life destroyed

My name is ISAIAH TORRES

JESSICA ♥ JACKSON

I'll let you know how to pick up your copy soon

(Royalties from my books go to Child Protection charities)

Acknowledgments

I could not be more grateful for the response and the support I received from my readers after Facebook suddenly banned my Page, and I lost all my Followers – thanks to you, we're getting back on track again.

But just as valued are those of you who don't use social media, and yet show your support in so many other ways.

Thanks also to my wonderful beta readers: Jackson, Linda and Roy M Burgess (an awesome crime author in his own right), and my ARC readers who come through for me time and again. And last, but not least, you – for reading and keeping the memory of each child alive.

Without the support of you amazing people, I would not still be writing.

Introduction

Beginning a new volume of Abused to Death brings mixed feelings.

There's hope that a new book will bring new readers and more awareness of children's suffering. But also sadness, because it reminds me that there are still many stories to be told.

I'm so glad you're helping me to keep these dreadful tragedies in people's minds, as we follow my ABCD mantra:

> A – Assume nothing
>
> B – Be vigilant
>
> C – Check everything
>
> D – Do something

And please, always listen to the children.

MY NAME IS CHILD B

My Name is Child B

And this is my story …

(Dear Reader, please turn back for a short message from the author, and information about your FREE ebook)

'When are you leaving?'

'In the morning, I think. Can you be there?'

'The whole gang'll be there,' says Freddie. 'My dad's going to give the three of us a lift. Do you know what time it'll be?'

'I'm not sure.'

'It's okay. Dad'll drop us off at nine. We can just wait around until we see you.' He nudges my shoulder. 'We'll all miss you, buddy.'

'I'm sorry.'

'It's not your fault. But I wish you weren't going.'

'Me too.'

I'm glad his bus comes before mine, and that he gets on board before he can spot me sniffing and wiping my eyes.

Get a grip, man! A new town. A new school. This could be a fantastic adventure!

MY NAME IS CHILD B

The next morning, I dawdle as much as I can, but by half past nine, Mom is losing it with me, saying how it's all my fault we're leaving town. I look up and down the road for the last time. Mom stuffs my bag into back of the van. I have to get in beside it, and I know I'm going to be bounced up and down all the way across state to Palermo.

'All set?' says Mom, turning the key in the ignition, as Freddie's dad's blue Jetta turns the corner.

'Mom, can we stop? Please.'

But she turns up the radio, and I look out the back window, as my best friends wave 'Goodbye'.

§

The new house is all on one level, and my sister and I each have our own space. But Mom is dumping a load of her extra stuff in my room, so I might not be able to get around as easily as I'd like. I wonder what the town's like, and the school. I'll miss my friends, but I have to look to the future, because we won't be going back.

Meeting new people can go one of three ways; they treat me like a half-wit and bully the life out of me, or they think I'm a sweet, little kid they can talk down to, or they're just as they'd be with any teenage kid they can have fun around. I'm aiming for that last one, so I'll put my swagger on, and it'll be the confident me who goes to school tomorrow.

The young woman scopes the yard, eyes darting from one child to another. When they finally rest on me, I give her a thumbs up and she comes over.

'What a morning,' she says, reaching out her hand.

I give her my firmest handshake. 'Tough day?'

'My little girl's sick. My mom's out of town, and I don't like to leave her with just anyone.'

'Try not to worry,' I say. 'I can guarantee your day's about to get a whole lot better.'

She breaks into a smile. 'Oh yeah?'

'Oh yeah. I'd put money on it.'

One of the supervisors strides over. 'You guys know where to go? You can't hang around in the yard all day.'

My new companion looks more anxious than ever.

'Hurry up and get where you need to be. And for goodness sake, do it before the bell rings.'

'We're fine,' I say, and catch the sigh of relief from somewhere around my right shoulder, as Mr Not-So-Welcoming hotfoots it towards a couple of kids who look as if they're about to get physical.

'Thanks,' she says. 'I don't know why I'm so nervous. Right, so where do we go?'

'Haven't a clue.'

She laughs. 'I suppose I should make sure – you're Jordan, right?'

'Last time I checked.'

'In case you haven't noticed, it's my first day as well.'

'No problem,' I say. 'Once I've learned the ropes I'll help you to settle in.'

She laughs again. 'Thanks. But aren't you nervous?'

'No, not really. Are you?'

'Yeah, I guess I am. A little. Do you find it easy to get to know new people?'

'I do, usually. But hey, don't worry. I'll be your wing-man. We've got this.'

'I bought this new outfit to give me confidence.'

I nod. She does look smart.

'I think I look cute today, do you?'

I raise an eyebrow. 'My, we're quite the narcissist, aren't we?'

Why don't I keep my big mouth shut? I know my sarcasm can be a bit much sometimes. But I look up at my new teaching assistant, and she's laughing.

'I think we're going to get along just fine,' she says.

'You betcha. What shall I call you?' I can see 'Miss Davies' on her name badge, but surnames are so formal.

'I prefer Kathi, if that's okay with you.'

Yep, she's right; we are definitely going to get along just fine.

The bus monitor lowers the ramp. 'How was your first day then?'

'Yeah, good. Everyone seems pretty nice. I reckon it'll do.'

Judy laughs. 'Oh, it's good enough for you, is it?'

'Just about.'

'Hurry up, JB, we're going to be late!' calls my new friend, Reece, from the sidewalk.

'Hang on, I'm busy!'

'Stop flirting with Judy; she prefers her guys tall and blond.'

'Like you, you mean.'

Judy makes sure I'm secure before hitting the button to lower the ramp again.

Reece bustles onto the bus and flops down beside me. He gives me a fist bump. 'You're not bad for the new kid on the block.'

We trade jibes until Reece gets off at his stop, and I have time to think. It's been the best day. I wasn't sure how things were going to go; some people take a while to get used to my dry sense of humour, but the last thing I want to do is hurt anyone's feelings.

Judy pulls up the bus at the bottom of our path, where Mom is leaning against the fence.

'You don't need to meet him off the bus, Mrs Waldron,' says Judy. 'I can make sure he gets right to the door.'

'Great,' says Mom.

Judy high fives me. 'See you tomorrow, handsome.'

The first week flies by, and before I know it, it's Monday morning again.

Kathi is waiting for me at the school gates. 'Ready for another day, Jordan?'

'You bet, Miss. Hoping to get more work done on my History project.'

'Hey, that's *our* project,' laughs Reece. 'And it's coming along pretty well, thanks to me.'

'A bit less laughing, you two, and you could be finished by the end of the week.'

'Yeah, but if we were quiet it'd be boring for the whole class.' I twist my head around to look at her. She's smiling; I knew she would be.

'I guess you're right. Okay, let's get you down to the nurse.'

'Hey, Miss Alvaro.'

'Hey, Jordan. And you know it's Evelyn. You get time for breakfast this morning?'

I'm on the verge of lying when my tummy rumbles.

'I guess not,' she smiles, and hands me a Quest bar. The pecan one; my favourite. 'How was your weekend?' she says, as she grabs the pack of wipes.

'Oh, y'know. So-so.'

'Watch the game on TV?'

'Wasn't it the best?'

'Shame they lost though.'

'Yeah, yeah I know, but still it was a good game.'

'Who's your favourite these days?'

'Farrell. He played a blinder on Saturday.'

'Hang on, Jordan. Farrell retired a couple of seasons ago.'

I blush. I don't want her to know I hardly get to watch TV at home. 'Well, yeah, but I still like him.'

'I understand, big guy.' She closes the cupboard. 'Right, all done. See you back here at afternoon recess?'

'Sure thing.'

'Kathi, we're done here.'

Miss Davies comes back into the nurses' office.

'His Lordship's ready to go to class now.'

'Thanks, Evelyn. Come on, Jordan, let's rock.'

'And roll,' I say. It makes her giggle.

§

I've been at Mexico School for so long now I feel like part of the furniture. Everything runs like clockwork, even with Reece and me messing around for laughs. Lunch-breaks are fun. Reece knows some great jokes and I goof around behind his back while he's telling them. But when Kathi comes in I'm happy to calm down and get something to eat. She takes me to the corner.

'I'm nearly ready to eat at the main table,' I say.

'You are? That's great. Want to do that tomorrow?'

'Sure, I'd love that,' I say. 'But can it be something I won't make a mess of?'

'You won't, Jordan.'

I glance at her.

'But I'll make sure you can manage.'

'Do you think I'll get the new chair they talked about, Kathi?'

'I sure hope so. You grew out of this one ages ago. But your mom needs to take you to the Doctor's office. Then they can prescribe one for you.'

'Mom hasn't taken me for a long time.'

'I'll remind her, Jordan.'

Another part of the routine comes at the end of each day, when one of the little kids hangs out with Reece and me while we're waiting for the bus.

'I'm going to marry you when I'm all grown up, Jordan,' she says most days.

'You are?'

'Yes, then I can take care of you and fix your broken legs.'

I laugh. 'But you're too young and cute for me.'

'You're cute too. I'm going to marry you.'

'Okay, sure. Will we go dancing together? When you've fixed my legs?'

'Of course. Mommy, Mommy!' A tall, curly-haired lady is coming across the yard. 'Mommy, Jordan said he'll marry me and we'll go dancing.'

'Did he, Poppet? You'd have a lot of fun together; that's for sure.'

The bus is pulling into its parking spot.

'See you tomorrow, Jordan.'

§

We're settling onto the front seats at the sports field. My school has a proud reputation to keep up, and although on wintry days it can get a bit cold, I wouldn't miss watching the hockey matches for the world. But I also have news for Kathi that can't wait.

'Hey, you did it! I'm going to get that new chair.'

She high fives me. 'That's great, Jordan.'

'I'll be able to change position myself.'

'Yep, you'll be much more comfortable. Those sores that started during the Christmas break still haven't quite gone away.'

'They're not so bad,' I fib. 'You and Evelyn are doing your best. And I guess I should've told the doctor about them.'

'You didn't tell him! Oh, Jordan!' She shakes her head. 'Never mind, we'll try and get your Mom to take you again.'

'Don't fuss, Kathi! Maybe I'll be able to go by myself in my new chair. With a joystick, I won't need to be pushed everywhere.'

She taps my shoulder. 'You'll be able to chase the girls more easily too!'

I glance over at Jenny at the far end of the bench. 'Well, I suppose so. If they play their cards right.'

Kathi nudges me. 'I've seen you two looking at each other.'

'She is pretty cute.'

'She is, Romeo. Let's hope you get that chair so you two can hang around together a bit more.'

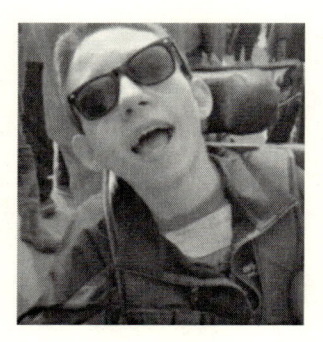

Jordan, the cool dude, having fun at school

Jenny realises we're watching her and blushes. Man, she looks cute when she does that.

'We've got the prescription from the doctor, so Mom just has to make an appointment with the sales people to get me measured up again.'

Kathi smiles, and for one awful moment I think she's going to tousle my hair. *I'm sixteen, Kathi, come on!* I duck slightly, just in case.

But she just tucks my blanket in a little tighter. 'That better, Jordan? It's really chilly out here.'

'Yeah, it's great,' I say, as we watch the players stride across the field towards the halfway line for the face-off. I feel a pang of regret, knowing I'll never be able to do what they do. Even wheelchair basketball's a bit of a stretch for me. The moment soon passes though. It is what it is.

Kathi nudges me again. 'She's coming over, Lover Boy.'

I flick my tongue across my teeth, relieved that Kathi brushed them this morning.

'Hey, JB.'

'Hey, Jenny.'

'Okay if I sit down here?'

'Sure,' says Kathi. 'I'll just pop across and see how Reece is doing.'

'Okay,' I say, half-glad she's leaving us alone, half-wishing she wasn't. My tongue decides to stick to the roof of my mouth, but I manage to croak. 'Your brother playing today, Jenny?'

'Yeah, first time out since that whack to his shin.'

'Maybe he'll get his own back on Travis today.'

'Yeah, maybe.' She twirls her hair between her fingers. 'I want to ask you something, Jordan.'

'Okay.'

'You know the Spring Dance is coming up at the end of the semester?'

I nod.

'I was just wondering …'

'Hey, Jenny.' Her friend is calling from the other end of the long bench. 'Come here a minute.'

'Can't it wait, Lynn?'

'What you saying?'

'Can't it wait?'

'No. Come on, it's an emergency. I just had a text from you-know-who.'

Jenny laughs. 'Looks like I'm needed. Catch you later, JB.'

'Sure, that'd be good.'

I sit on my own for a while. I don't mind. But it's hard to concentrate on the match when I'm wondering if Jenny's going to ask me to go to the dance with her. She looks over at me, only half-listening to Lynn. She pushes her sunglasses a bit further up her nose, and gives me an almost imperceptible thumbs up. *Oh my God, does she really like me?* I give her a thumbs up back, and she smiles, and my tummy turns over. *Oh my God, do I have a girlfriend? Okay, okay, stay cool.* If we go to the dance, I'm going to kiss her. And flowers. I'll buy her flowers. If Mom lets me go. And maybe I could have a new shirt. That would be awesome. *Will Mom let me go?* I say a little prayer.

Kathi comes back and takes her seat beside me. 'All good, Romeo?'

'I sure hope so. Now can we just watch the game!'

On the way back into school I tell Kathi my plan to become a teacher's aide. Just like her. Well, maybe not exactly like her. The physical stuff might be out of my league, but I can help the kids who need a bit of support.

She leans down and hugs me. 'You'll be amazing. I'll help you, Jordan.'

Wow. Just wow. I might have a girlfriend, I'm getting a new chair, and I have a career to aim for.

Life is so good right now.

§

Jenny and me don't get chance to talk over the next couple of days, but there's plenty of time.

On Thursday, before afternoon recess, Mr James gathers all the students around him. His face looks kinda grey, like he's just had some bad news. Kathi takes me to my place at the side so I can hear what he's saying.
    'Some of you will have heard of the Covid-19 virus that's sweeping around the world.'

Well yeah, I know about the virus, but it's mostly in China, with very few cases in the good old U. S. of A. I just want to get back to the project Reece and me are going to win first prize with. Well, maybe not first; but it'll be up there.
    'It's a little more dangerous than the President first thought, and now County have told us we have to temporarily shut down the school.'
    What! The cases in NY state have mostly been seniors, not school-kids.

A murmur goes around the room, and the word 'No!' is out of my mouth before I can stop it. I turn to Kathi, whose face matches Mr James'.

You can't shut down the school! 'No.' I whisper it this time.

'I know this is bad news for most of us, although some may be glad not to come into school for a little while,' continues Mr James, looking at Lonie Cooper, who's grinning his face off.

'It might only be for a week or two,' he goes on. 'We'll just have to wait and see. But you don't get off lightly. We'll be sending work for you to do at home, and a lot of it will need to be done on computer.'

I look at Kathi again. I don't have a computer. So she'll have to come by my house and help me. I don't know what Mom and Dad will have to say about that.

'And I'm afraid you won't be able to work one-on-one anymore.'

Reece's hand shoots up. 'But why, Sir?'

'We have to keep away from each other to stop the virus spreading,' says Mr James. 'So all teachers and aides will be doing work from their own homes, preparing lessons for you to do online.'

Kathi squeezes my shoulder. 'We'll sort something, Jordan.'

'I'm so sorry it's come to this,' says Mr James. 'I don't like it any more than you do. It's going to be tough on all of us.'

I swallow hard. No school. For at least a week. Just like in the holidays. But I can do this. I guess I have to.

Kathi raises her hand. 'What about the kids who need extra care?'

He shakes his head. 'I don't know yet, Miss Davies.'

'Can we go and help out at their homes?'

'No, that won't be allowed, I'm afraid.'

Kathi squats down beside me. 'I'm sorry, Jordan. Hey, I'll miss you.'

'It's okay, Kathi. It won't be for long.'

'Does anyone have any more questions?' says Mr James.

'When can we come back to school?' I say.

'The honest answer is that I don't know, Jordan. I'll be working on it though. Right, kids. The buses are waiting to take you home now.'

Now! So it's started already.

Kathi takes my hand as the other kids start heading outside.

'Hey, why don't I stay with you, Kathi? Then we can carry on as usual.' Even as I speak the words, I know it's a dumb thing to say.

'If only,' she says, and she has tears in her eyes.

Mr James comes over to join us. 'I can see you're worried, Miss Davies. But our hands are tied.'

'Can't we make a special case for Jordan? You know what happens when he stays home.'

'I know, I know. But it's a legal thing. We aren't allowed to mix with people outside our families.'

Kathi snorts. 'Family!'

'Let's get Jordan onto the bus, Kathi. Hey, this hiccup'll be over in no time.'

I say a silent prayer that it will be.

§

'What's going on?' says Mom, as Kathi wheels me up the path.

'Covid rules. No school until further notice.'

'Well, what the hell am I supposed to do with him?'

I don't think she means that as bad as it sounds. She's just stressed out at the moment, and now I'm gonna add to her troubles.

'I won't be any bother, Mom.'

She folds her arms. 'You'd better not be.'

'I'll be bringing work for him,' says Kathi. 'And we'll try and get a computer sorted.'

'What's the point?' says Mom. 'He's too stupid to learn anything.'

'You know that's not true, Mrs Waldron. Jordan was up for a class prize this Friday.'

Mom laughs. 'For what? Least improved student?'

Kathi grits her teeth. 'A little encouragement wouldn't go amiss.'

Mom gets right up in Kathi's face. 'You trying to tell me you know better than his own mother?'

Kathi is gentle. The sort of person who catches spiders under a drinking glass, then takes them outside to free them. She's not gentle right now. 'I do know that he's a clever boy, and he's happy in school. He just needs a bit of support at home to really shine.'

Mom scoffs and turns her back on us. 'Bring him into the hall.'

'But it's lovely out,' says Kathi. 'A bit of fresh air might put some colour in his cheeks. Besides, isn't it always stifling in your hallway when the sun shines?'

She's got that right. And freezing every other day. I hate being left there.

'You been complaining to the teacher, Jordan?'

'No, Mom. Unless I maybe mentioned it once.'

'Don't blame Jordan, Mrs Waldron.'

Mom gets right back up in Kathi's face. 'Right, you heard me, Classroom Aide,' Mom spits out. 'In the hall. Then take your sorry ass back where you came from.'

I'm still here when my stepdad gets home.

He kicks my chair as he squeezes past. I don't think it's deliberate, but it hurts just the same where my sores rub against the sides.

'He do something?'

'Just the usual,' says Mom. 'Sitting there, doing nothing. Getting on my nerves.'

My stepdad catches her in a hug. 'Aww, honey. You work too hard. You should put him outside where you don't have to see him.'

Now they want to put me outside. Now that it's dark and cold.

'Would you do it, Tony? I'll get on with supper.'

My stepdad bumps my chair down the step, and I try to stifle a cry of pain. I'm sure my bones must be poking through the skin.

'You'd better shut the fuck up, Jordan. Your mom and me have had just about enough of you.'

'I'm sorry, Dad.' Although I don't know what I'm supposed to be sorry for. Existing, I guess.

He turns the chair around so that I'm facing the door. 'You've made her mad today, boy.'

'I don't think I did anything wrong, Dad. The school is making us stay home, so I guess Mom is sore about that.'

'What's that you're saying, Retard? Can't you learn to speak properly? I was out earning my living at 16, and here you are, slavering and shaking like a baby in its buggy.'

There's nothing I can say. Because he's right. I'd give anything to have a job and my own apartment, maybe with Jenny by my side. But instead I'm stuck here, annoying everyone.

He goes inside and slams the door before I can ask for my jacket. Or a blanket.

I think about my stepdad and how tough it's been for him since the traffic accident. He was injured quite badly and had to stay in the hospital for a spell. When he couldn't get around so easy, I used to wish it'd make him understand how things are for me a little more. But I don't think it did. And then I felt mean for thinking that way. Anyway, he's recovered a whole lot now.

I don't know whether it's the cold, or knowing I won't be in school for a few days, or the way my legs are seizing up, but I let a few tears fall down my cheeks. I don't like to admit it, but deep down I know I'm crying because, unlike how it's been for Tony, there's no getting better for me. Even when I get my new wheelchair, I'll be using it for ever; I'll never be able to walk. I don't usually mind so much. As they say, it is what it is, and usually I'm fine about it. But there's something about that March night that's got me frustrated and upset. It'll be better when I next see Kathi. We can always make each other laugh.

I'm in the hall when she knocks on the door the next day.

'Mom, Mom, I think it's Kathi.'

'That bloody woman,' mutters Mom, as she shoves my chair out of the way. 'What the hell does she want?'

'Hi, Mrs Waldron.' Kathi cranes her neck past Mom. 'Hi buddy, how's it going? I brought you some stuff to read until we can get the computer set up.'

Mom scoffs. 'You think he's gonna trouble himself to read when he hasn't got you breathing down his neck?'

'I like to read, Mom. You know that.'

'Perhaps I could come in, Mrs Waldron. I've brought a new book-stand to replace the one that went missing. I can get it set up, and Jordan can carry on with his studies right away.'

'Uhm, no, Miss Davies. You don't need to come into my house. I'll take whatever you've brought and we'll set it up ourselves.'

'But the last time you said it was too difficult, and Jordan couldn't do his homework for weeks.'

'We'll be just fine. I'm sure you have other places to go.'

'It'll only take a minute, and I'd love to have a little chat with Jordan.'

'He's not feeling too well today. Isn't that right, Jordan?'

'But Mom, I …'

A glare from my mom stops me in my tracks. 'Well no, I guess I don't feel so good.'

'You sure, Jordan?'

'He's sure. Now, if there's nothing else?' Mom holds out her hands to take the books and the stand.

'I'll be back tomorrow,' says Kathi. 'I'd sure like to see Jordan then, and see how his studies are going.'

'Yeah, yeah. Let's wait and see.' Mom is closing the door in Kathi's face.

'See you tomorrow, Jordan. And we'll soon have that computer set up for you.'

'Bye, Kathi,' I shout as loudly as I can through the closed door.

I hear Mom on the phone the next day.

'Sure, that's no problem. He doesn't need anyone anyway. No, no, that's fine. Don't give it another thought. He's not going anywhere.' She laughs at her joke. 'Whenever you can. Yes, that's great. Thank you.' She puts down the phone. 'Well, that's that, then.'

'What, Mom?'

'Your beloved teacher. She can't come after all. Not for a while anyway. Covid rules. Right let's get you outside; you absolutely stink.'

'My diaper, Mom. Maybe you could change it.'

'Oh, shut up, Jordan.'

'Hey, Jordy.'

'Hey, Mrs Price. Hey, Scruffy.'

The aptly-named puppy dashes up to greet me, and I reach down to scratch behind his ears.

'You taking in the night air again, Jordy?'

'Sure am. It's real peaceful out here in the evenings.'

'A little chilly though, don't you think?'

'Just a bit. But I don't feel the cold.' That's not exactly true, but to be fair on Mom, she does sometimes wrap my comforter around me, so it's not so bad.

'Strong fella,' she smiles. 'But in case you feel like something extra to keep you warm, I got a little blanket right here.' She fishes the red-checked cover out of her bag, and I look at it longingly.

'I'm just fine, Mrs Price. But thank you.'

'You're shivering, Jordy. Please put it over your legs for a spell.'

I glance up at the window. 'Well, I guess it won't hurt none. Not too tight though.' I'll need to take it off myself when Mom or my stepdad come out to get me.

She tucks the blanket loosely over me. 'There now, much better. Want me to turn you round so you can see the cars and people coming and going?'

'Oh no, I like it better this way. It's my thinking time. You remember I told you I'm going to be a teacher?'

'I sure do, Jordy.'

'Well, I do all kinds of planning when I sit out here in the evenings. What lessons I'll teach, how I'll help the ones who aren't quick to learn, maybe have an after-school club with milk and cookies.'

'Oh, that reminds me,' says Mrs Price. More fishing in the bag. 'I made these just now; they're still warm.' She breaks the cookie into pieces, and we munch together. Even Scruffy gets his share.

'I wish I could make cookies for you, Mrs Price.'

'Maybe one day.'

It's nice of her to think that way, but I look down at my hands and know I never will.

'I like what you said about becoming a teacher. My late husband was a teacher too.'

'No way!'

'Yes way,' she laughs. 'He …'

We both start at a noise behind the front door.

Mrs Price grabs the blanket and I lick the crumbs from around my lips, as I watch my friend and Scruffy hurry away.

'I heard talking,' says my stepdad.

I don't answer. He might let it pass.

'Don't be telling anyone our business. You got that?'

'Yes, Sir.'

'Mom says to bring you in now. You can watch some TV.'

The relief washes over me, and I take my chance. 'Could I maybe have a bite to eat, and have my diaper changed?'

'Don't push it, Buster.'

I'm not sleeping too well. I do have a bed, but sometimes my mom and stepdad are too tired to put me in there at night-time. This is one of those nights.

'Could I have my comforter please, Mom?' It doesn't block the draught completely, but it's way better than nothing to keep out the worst of the cold as I sit in the hallway.

'Goodness, Jordan, can't you see I'm busy?'

More than the blanket, more than food or something to drink, I long to have my diaper changed. I'm used to the smell of course, but the sticky dirtiness I feel seems to seep into my pores, and I want to cry with frustration. When Nurse Evelyn used to change it at school, it was over in a flash, but when Mom does it she huffs and puffs and it seems to take forever.

I wake up in the middle of the night. I know that the shadows that used to terrify me when I was younger aren't coming to get me. I know that the creaking sounds are just the house 'settling down', and that the thumping, far from being the sneaking tread of a monster, is just the sound of my heart beating in my ears.

But still, I cry. I'm 16 years old, almost 17, almost a man, but I cry during the long nights. I pray for the strength in my body to adjust my position, just a little bit. I shift slightly, but the pain from my sores is unbearable. The wet, goopy mess I'm sitting in settles into the open wounds and I know I'm trapped in this cycle of filth and pain, for who knows how long. I hope Kathi will be allowed to come see me soon.

§

I try to listen to the news as the sound creeps under the living room door and out into the hallway.

There's a world pandemic of the virus. It spreads through bodily contact, so everyone has to keep that to a minimum, and wear surgical-style masks when they go out to meet other people.

Folks all over the world are dying from the disease that attacks the lungs and stops you from breathing. Hospitals are overwhelmed with cases, and seniors and people with certain health conditions, are the most at risk. I'm pretty sure that my cerebral palsy doesn't give me an increased chance of acquiring the coughing and breathlessness that befalls most victims. But as I tilt more and more to the side in my chair, without Kathi or Evelyn or anyone to sit me up straight again, I'm starting to get out of breath.

Recently, I've been spending most of the time here in the hallway. I've stopped asking Mom to change my diaper, cos it seemed like she was deliberately ignoring my pleading, and that hurt as much as the agony of the sores.

Sometimes, I hear Scruffy barking as Mrs Price goes past our door. She knocks one day, and Mom pushes me into the living room and warns me to be quiet.

'I haven't seen Jordan for a while, Lisa. Is he okay?'

'Oh, he's fine. You know Jordan. He's just in the bath right now, but I'll tell him you dropped by.'

'I'm glad he's okay. I'll call again tomorrow, shall I?'

'Well, you know we're not supposed to mix with each other. So better not. But thank you.'

Mrs Price does knock again the next day, and when she tries the day after that, Mom tells her I'm sick with the virus and shouldn't be disturbed. I hear Mrs Price say, 'Send Jordan my love,' and my heart skips a beat. Love, such a short, easy word. But it means so much. When this is over, I'm going to tell Kathi and Reece and Jenny that I love them.

§

Kathi has come back. I knew she'd come as soon as she could. Mom even lets her through the door.

'Look what I've got!' She pushes a few magazines and plates to the side, and places a laptop on the table.

'Wow!'

'Hang on a minute,' says Mom. 'We haven't got room for that.'

'I'm afraid it's a legal requirement, Mrs Waldron. Kids still have to learn.'

Mom shrugs. 'As long as it doesn't get in the way then.'

'It won't, Mom. I promise.'

'And how the hell are you going to make sure of that? You gonna lift the damn thing off the table with your no-good arms?'

I cringe. I don't like Kathi to see how Mom talks to me. So I laugh. 'Yeah, I guess so!'

'Jordan won't need that book-stand now,' says Kathi. 'I'll take it back and put it into our stationery store.'

Mom's as quick as a whip. 'He broke the darn thing, didn't you, Jordan? Had to put it in the trash.'

Kathi gives Mom the same look she gave Reece and me when we told her it wasn't us who hid Macie's lunchbox behind the chalkboard. 'That's okay.' Her jaw is clenched, like she's holding back from cussing. 'He's got the computer now. We'll be checking in with him on camera to make sure everything's running smoothly.' She looks around for a plug socket.

I point to the wall behind us.

'Thanks, Jordan. Right, let me show you how it all works. Carol and Wanda will be checking in with you too, so we'll be keeping you busy.'

'Great!' I say. I miss my physical therapist and occupational therapist almost as much as I miss Kathi.

'Lisa, while I'm here, can I give you a hand with changing Jordan's diaper?'

'No, don't you worry about that. I can manage just fine. I'll let you get on and visit your other students.'

'Oh no, I'm in no hurry. I'd love to stay and chat with Jordan.'

'He's getting tired. Look how he's flopping over to the side.'

'I can get him upright, Mrs Waldron.'

'No.' Mom is firmer this time. 'He's tired and you need to go.'

Kathi leans down to hug me. 'You okay, big man?' she whispers.

'I'm fine.'

'I think you need some more help,' she whispers.

'Maybe,' I say.

'Right, I'll get going then, Mrs Waldron. You all take care now.'

§

I haven't heard Scruffy for a while. Mrs Price should still be walking him like always. Unless we're not even allowed to do things like that now. I think of Scruffy's wagging tail as he jumps up to greet me, and his excited barking when Mrs Price gives him a treat. I even think of his yelping that day he accidentally got locked in our back yard, and his head got caught in the fence as he tried to escape.

When I don't hear them for the longest time, in my heart I know, before I even hear Mom and Dad talking.

'She's the second person,' says Dad. 'There's Tony's granddad too.'

'And that kid. The one with the asthma.'

'I forgot about her. That's three that we know of.'

'I wonder what'll happen to that damn dog,' says Mom.

That night I pray for Mrs Price to get to heaven, although I know she will, and that Scruffy will get somebody to love and care for him as much as she did.

§

I still try to think about what I'll do when I get back to school. I'll joke with Judy as she helps me onto the bus. Mr James and Miss Davies will welcome us all back, and I'll laugh and tease my classmates again. Reece and I will finish our latest project, and everyone will think it's great! We'll give a little presentation at the next Parents' Evening, and although Mom and Dad won't go, Reece's Mom and Stepdad, and all the other parents will clap and be proud of us. Sometimes I pretend Mom and Dad do show up, and are so proud of me, and they join in with the clapping.

The Spring Dance was cancelled long ago, and I have no clue what Jenny's doing now. She's one of the clever kids, and she'll be going to college soon. I hope she doesn't move far away. I hope she doesn't get a boyfriend. If only I'd had the chance to kiss her. Just once. It's a kind of dream of mine to know how it feels to kiss a girl. I guess it's soft and warm and sexy.

§

When I'm not so tired, I think about how it'll be when I'm a teacher. I've decided I could do a lot to help kids like me. Those who have extra needs, but don't get them met at home. I've got a ton of ideas.

But mostly I try to make my mind go blank, because the pain is so bad now. Even Mom looked shocked when she last changed my diaper and the sores were running with pus and my flesh was eaten away to the bone.

'Maybe we could go to the doctor, Mom.'

Once the clean diaper is back on, she seems to forget how bad it is. 'We can't, Jordan. Stop complaining about it. A few sores won't do you any harm.'

'Or we could get some more of the cream. That used to help a lot.'

'Shut up about it, can't you? You're not the only one got problems, you know.'

'I know, Mom. I'm sorry. But please will you think about it. I really don't feel too good.'

§

I'm scared the sores are becoming infected, and I know that's going to affect the rest of my body. I can't think like I used to, and I just feel sick. It's hard to describe it; like all the life is being sucked out of me, and my skin is empty. Like there's nothing inside.

I don't bother talking much anymore. Without Kathi or Reece or Mrs Price and Scruffy, or any of my other friends to chat to, there doesn't seem to be any point. When Mom and Tony have to go out to the store or wherever we're allowed to go these days, they squeeze past me in the hallway without saying a word. So I only speak when I have to, and my voice is getting hoarse. And to be honest, a bit like with my thoughts, I can't seem to make any sense with my words.

I still manage to pray sometimes. I pray that no more people die of this thing, and that it'll go away and I can get back to school.

'Jordan, can you turn on the camera for today's session?'

'I can't, Miss Davies. It's still broken.'

'My, your voice is croaky, Mister. Can you put your mom or dad on, then? We might be able to fix it.'

Mom is glaring at me and shaking her head.

'I'm sorry. They're both busy right now.'

'Your breathing sounds a little off, Jordan. Have you been able to sit up straight?'

Mom will kill me if I make Kathi think I'm not okay. 'Sure. I've just been doing a few exercises. You know I get breathless when I do them.'

'I've been trying to get help for you, Jordan. Did anyone come?'

'Nobody came, Miss,' I whisper. Mom's still within earshot.

'I'll try again. And I'll come and see you.'

'No, you can't do that.'

Mom leans into the microphone. 'You need to obey the rules, Miss Davies. No home visits.'

'But I'm worried about him, Lisa.'

'He's fine. You're fine, aren't you, Jordan?'

I feel worn out. I want to sleep. 'Yes, I'm fine, Mom. Just a little tired.'

'You've exhausted him,' says Mom. 'You're supposed to help him, but you're making him worse.'

'Please let me visit, Lisa.'

'We'll see. Maybe in a few days. It's time to end the call now. Say 'Goodbye' to your teacher, Jordan.'

'Thank you for helping me, Kathi.'

'I'll see you soon, Jordan. I promise.'

As the call ends, I turn to Mom. 'I hurt real bad, Mom. Please can you change my diaper? And maybe I could have a sponge bath.'

'Oh, shut up, Jordan. It's not all about you.'

And I have to continue to sit in my filth, more and more of it every day. And I can't move any part of my body anymore to take the pressure off my rigid, agonising limbs.

§

I'm outside at last. And I'm grateful, because the sun is warm, and I can hear the birds singing. If Kathi knew I was out here, she could come visit with me. And we could laugh like we used to. And gossip. Kathi used to say I was a busybody at times. She's right, of course; I did love to chat. I wonder when we can get back to school and everything will be good again.

The bad thing about being outside though, is that the hens from some of the other houses on the street come clucking around me. I can't shoo them away like I used to, and they've recently taken an interest in the sores on my legs. At first, they just sniffed around, but lately they've started pecking at the blood and pus that comes out of them. The sores already hurt real bad, but the sharpness of their beaks jabbing at my skin is agony.

Sometimes the neighbourhood kids help me out, and clap their hands to make the hens run away. One little fella sticks around to talk a while.

'How come you sit outside in the sun, Mr Jordan?'

'Well, I like it.' It's strange to hear the sound of my rasping voice.

'You do? It gets kinda hot about midday.'

'I know, but I don't mind it.'

'But you can get out from that chair and walk around if you want to, right?'

He's a sweet kid, and I don't want to lie to him. I shake my head. 'No, but I'm okay.'

'You don't look okay, Mr Jordan. Can't you sit up straight like you used to?'

'Not so much.'

'Mr Jordan?'

'Yeah?'

'You don't smell so good.'

I blush right down to the roots of my hair. 'I guess.'

'My mom says you can't get washed all by yourself like I can.'

'Your mom is right. But my mom washes me.'

'Well, I reckon she's overdue on that.'

I smile. 'I reckon she is.'

'You sure you're okay, Mr Jordan?'

This little kid cares more about me than Mom. 'I'm sure.'

'My big brother could push you and we could go to the park. We could even go the mall. He's got his driver's licence now.'

'He has? That's great. But we'd better not. My mom wouldn't like it.'

'Oh, she sounds as bad as mine. Always wants to know where I am. Every minute. She'll be yelling for me soon.'

'Yeah, I guess.'

'It's because they love us, Mr Jordan. Not because they're being mean.'

I nod. I really want to believe that.

The chickens are strutting back towards us, and the little boy shoos them away again.

'Wade! Wade, you come back in now!'

'Told you,' says Wade, with a shrug. 'I don't mind though. It's ice cream for dessert today. See you, Mr Jordan.'

'See you, Wade.' And I imagine the coolness of blueberry ice cream sliding down my parched throat, as the chickens crowd in and peck at my sores.

I'm even more worried than before about the sores on my legs, not to mention in the other places. I remember hearing Nurse Evelyn telling Kathi that we had to watch out for them getting infected, cos that can cause real problems. She explained that keeping my skin clean was very important, and that leaving a dirty diaper on was a terrible risk.

That was back when my diaper was only left on over the weekend. In those days, Mom would change it a few times during the school holidays, so it wasn't too bad. But now, it's been weeks and weeks. I guess it could even have been months. I'm getting all confused.

§

'Well, I just can't do it,' says Mom. 'It sticks to his skin and I can't get it off.'

'You're not trying hard enough. Here, I'll do it.'

Tony begins to rip the diaper off my skin, but I scream so loudly the neighbour comes to our door. 'What's going on in there? Sounds like you're hurting the boy.'

'Everything's fine,' says Tony, as I shiver and whimper like a baby.

'Jordan,' yells the neighbour. 'You okay, son?'

'He's fine,' says Mom. 'Go away.'

'He doesn't sound fine. I'm going to get him some help.'

It goes quiet. I guess the neighbour has gone.

My whole body is trembling like crazy, and my arms are flailing around as if they have a mind of their own.

'What the hell's he doing?' says Tony.

'I don't know. But I think he's sick.'

'He'd better not have caught the virus and brought it into our home.'

'How could he? He hasn't been anywhere.'

'He has those kids coming around, doesn't he?'

'Tell the kids to go away when they bother you, son. Okay?'

'Mom,' I mumble. 'Mom, help me.'

'Shut up, Jordan,' says Tony.

'No, he's sick. Look at the colour of his face.'

'He's always white.'

'No, he's grey now, and clammy. And his lips are blue.'

My limbs are still jerking, each spasm escalating the pain. I'm in unbearable agony when I move, but I can't stop. 'Somebody, please help me.' After a while, the spasms recede and I flop backwards, my head dropping to my chest. Mom and Tony have gone into the kitchen. The smell of frying burgers makes me throw up down my front. Some of it sticks in my throat.

'Put him back in the bedroom. Let him sleep it off,' says Tony.

'Don't leave me.'

'What's he saying?'

'I don't know. But look at his tongue. It's blue as well now. And why won't that rash go?'

'Stop worrying, woman. We'll get him to the doctor's office next week.'

'That fever is getting worse. We need help.'

'You need to rest, Lisa. All this worrying is going to make you more sick than the boy.'

'Okay, okay.' I feel a touch on my forehead. The most gentle touch I've felt in weeks. 'Go to sleep, Jordan. I'll come back and see you in a little while.'

'Mom, don't go.' But no one can hear me.

§

When they lifted me onto the bed yesterday I screamed and squirmed and sobbed so hard they almost dropped me on the floor. I fainted in agony.

This morning, Mom brought the little TV into my room and placed it on the cabinet at the foot of my bed. And I guess I've gone through the pain barrier into a sort of delirium where things seem quite funny. There's an old Marx brothers film playing. A Night at the Opera. I watched it at Reece's house once; he can do Groucho to a T. My throat is too dry to make any sort of noise, and I can hardly see, but inside I'm kind of smiling.

Someone is banging on the door.

'Let us see him, Lisa. We can help you.'

'Leave us alone. We don't want your help.'

Lots of talking and yelling.

'Please take him to the doctor, Lisa.'

'He's my kid, I'll decide that.'

The door slams.

'Okay, I'm calling the cops.'

I don't know who that was and I don't know if the cops come or not.

My thoughts are jumbled all the time; nothing makes any sense. I'm running with sweat and trembling with the cold. I can hardly breathe, and the pain is back. Every few minutes I lose consciousness, and when I wake up I'm scared I'm losing my mind. I don't think they've tried to feed me or change my diaper for a while, but I'm not sure I'm soiling it much anymore. I just don't know. The pain in my back is excruciating. *What's happening to me?*

§

'Jordan, come on. Wake up.'

'Leave him if he wants to sleep.'

'Jordan, Jordan! I don't think he's asleep.'

'He must be. Let him rest.'

'No, he's not asleep. I'm sure he's not. Jordan, Jordan! You need to wake up.'

'This is crazy. I'm going out.'

'No, don't go! Can't you see he's not just sleeping?'

'What then? Okay, let me see.'
'He's not moving.'
'Well, he can't move, can he?'
'This is different. Look at him. Touch his skin.'
'It's clammy, I guess.'
'And his eyes. He hasn't blinked this whole time.'
'Oh, fucking hell, Lisa.'
'I'm right, aren't I?'
'I think so. What the hell are we going to do?'

§

My name is Jordan Brooks

And I was 17 years old

When I was neglected to death

Thank you for reading my story

Please don't forget me

I was alerted to Jordan's case by one of the readers who has been with me since the very beginning. Set near where she lives, Susan was keen to let me know of the fate of the teenage boy with a wicked sense of humour, and an infectious smile.

Before we continue with the story, and go deeper into the case, please don't miss the following ...

Invitation To My Readers' List

I'd love you to enjoy the benefits of my Readers' List, including: each new release at the subscriber price, the chance to win a **personally signed paperback book,** special offers on similar books, and lots more.

> **Please add my email address to your VIP/ Primary/ Favourites/ Priority/ Focused/ contacts:**
> **jessicajackson@jesstruecrime.com**

Then join in 2 easy steps:

1) Scan the code overleaf for your FREE ebook

2) Click YES in the email I'll send you, **after around 3 minutes**, to confirm your place

> *Please respond to confirm your place, as without it, I'm so sorry but I can't include you, so check all mailboxes, including Spam.*

Pick Up Your Free Book

Don't miss the story of Isaiah Torres – abused to death in the most appalling way.

1) Get your book

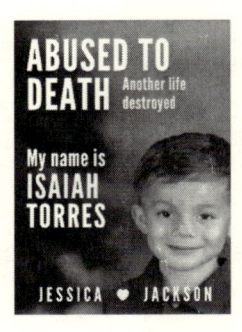

Just scan this code:

Or use this link:

https://BookHip.com/KXACJDT

2) Click in the email to confirm your place

If You Need A Little Help

Technology can be a pain, so if you have any problems downloading your ebook – don't worry, help is right there for you.

Just click **Need Help** at the top right of the screen:

(Or if you're really stuck, email me, and I'll be happy to add you manually.)

jessicajackson@jesstruecrime.com

Enter My Draw

The next 2 steps are optional, but they give you the chance to win a free, signed paperback book.

Once you've **confirmed your place** and joined us, I'll email you with the question: "Are They Monsters?" I'd love to know your opinion and add it to my poll, so when you receive it …

3) Click your choice in the email

The day after you send me your choice, I'll email with your invitation to enter the draw for a personally signed paperback book; UNIQUE only to winners of the draw.

So be sure to …

4) Say YES to enter the draw

Good luck!

And by the way …

Thanks To You

When you buy one of my books, read pages in KU, write a review, or tell your friends about my books, you are not only helping to raise awareness, but to raise money for child protection charities.

I donate a portion of the royalties from my books to these two charities:

– NSPCC (UK)
– UNICEF (worldwide)

Let's carry on ...

MY NAME IS CHILD B

JESSICA JACKSON

The Murder of Jordan Brooks

Jordan Brooks
23 November 2003 – 9 May 2021
aged 17 years & 6 months
Oswego County, New York State

Jordan Brooks (sometimes referred to as Jordan Motto, which is his mother's maiden name) was born in November 20003, with the disability, cerebral palsy. This condition usually means that the brain (*cerebral*) was affected before, during or soon after birth, often after being deprived of oxygen. The resultant *palsy*, which means weakness or issues with using the muscles, often affects the child's movement and fine motor skills, sometimes including speech and mobility. Like most people with this disability, Jordan nevertheless was a bright, intelligent boy, with a keen sense of humour.

Little has been documented about Jordan's life until 2018, at which time the family settled in Palermo, Oswego County, New York State, where he attended Mexico School. He had a younger sister, 13 at the time of her brother's death, who spent much of her time at a friend's home. I also gather that Jordan's birth father was dead.

Between the years 2012 to 2017, before the family moved to Palermo, there were five F.A.R. (Family Assessment Response) investigations, as a result of allegations of Lack of Medical Care, Excessive Corporal Punishment, Inadequate Guardianship, Lacerations/ Bruises/ Welts, and Inadequate Food/ Clothing/ Shelter. Whilst you and I might be alarmed, and feel that these allegations warrant serious intervention, it was felt that the Brooks/ Waldron children did not meet the criteria (of serious child abuse and immediate danger) to warrant this, and Child Protection workers instead opted to work with the family to resolve the issues.

I have summarised the description of Family Assessment Response from New York State Office of Children and Family Services' website:

> A Family Assessment Response (FAR) is used when it is felt that a full investigation into allegations of child maltreatment is not

> required. This alternative approach provides protection to children by engaging families in an assessment of child safety and of family needs, in finding solutions to family problems and in identifying informal and formal supports to meet their needs and increase their ability to care for their children.

I'm sure this type of response works very well on many, many occasions, and I am in strong support of helping families to learn how to be more aware of their child's needs, and parent effectively. Tragically, as his caregivers were so resistant to supporting him, this did not help Jordan.

Although, at that time, Jordan was of normal weight, did not have the appalling sores that blighted his later years, and was better able to swallow, etc, with at least five reports made to the authorities of what to you and I are horrifying allegations, their conclusion not to act more decisively put Jordan in harm's way.

At that point, the Waldrons had suffered very few consequences for the abuse they dealt to their son, but I assume they were growing angry at the interference in their family affairs. So, although I have not found concrete proof of this, the Waldrons may have moved house, as many do, when they felt the heat of child protective services on their necks.

§

I have used the pseudonym Kathi Davies for Jordan's Teaching Assistant, who began her new job on the same day that Jordan, the pupil she was assigned to work with, also had his first day at the school. She found Jordan to be "a happy kid" who, although he was a joker, with a sarcastic turn of wit, cared about his friends and was extremely helpful. I will continue to use the name Kathi Davies in this part of the book.

> I have tried, without success, various avenues to make contact with this lovely lady, as she seems to have had a close bond with Jordan, and the pictures with him on her Facebook profile are beautifully poignant. I would love to name-check this lady and celebrate her wonderful relationship with Jordan, showing photographs of she and Jordan together, but I hope she will not mind that I have included some of her photographs showing just Jordan.

Similarly, Jordan's physical therapist, occupational therapist, bus monitor, and many others, brought him happiness and support.

Ms Davies worked with Jordan for the three years leading up to his death. She assisted the teenager with his food, changing his diapers, and taking him to various healthcare appointments. Before his health began to severely deteriorate, Jordan took part in many school activities, including the Special Olympics. But Kathi began to notice that Jordan didn't seem to be bathed regularly, nor did he have his teeth brushed; a task she took on with Lisa Waldron's consent.

An important part of Ms Davies' role was ensuring that Jordan was moved in his wheelchair on an hourly basis, thereby mitigating the incidence of pressure sores. But she and his physical therapist became aware that it was increasingly difficult to stretch him, particularly after weekends or school holidays at home, indicating that he was not being sufficiently stretched or moved, in or from his wheelchair, during these times. They also spotted pressure sores, including one the size of a baseball.

As a young man with a physical disability, Jordan's dignity was neglected, and his white wheelchair cushion had become blackened and stank of urine. School staff pitched in by buying a new cushion, washing and swapping the old and new around so that a clean one was always readily available.

When Jordan's time with the caregivers at his school was dwarfed by the time at the family home, his tilted body position became much more pronounced, and his ability to swallow was further compromised, meaning that he had to take strong gulps to make food and liquid go down.

During the coronavirus pandemic, like many schools worldwide, the children were not permitted to attend, as it was felt that schools were potential breeding grounds for the deadly virus. Educators were tasked with implementing virtual learning programs.

§

Despite lockdown, Kathi Davies made a number of visits to Jordan's home, out of concern for her much-loved pupil, and because she simply missed him. But she must have been upset to see Jordan's further deterioration, as he grew thinner, his oral hygiene suffering from lack of teeth cleaning, and she noticed a new, pungent odour about him.

His attendance at virtual school sessions gradually dwindled, and Lisa Waldron frequently cancelled the appointments with health practitioners that could have resulted in making her son more comfortable.

Heartbreakingly, Davies later testified in court that Jordan had begun to look extremely frail, and that, when sitting outside his home, chickens had been pecking at the sores on his legs.

6 May 2021 was the last day that Kathi spoke to Jordan during a virtual session, and she noted that his breathing was laboured. This caring woman, who had built up such a strong bond with Jordan, and had reported his case to CPS on several occasions, must have felt helpless, hearing his breathlessness and distress. His camera was often turned off, as it was on this occasion, so she couldn't even see him. Jordan died three days later.

§

Along with Kathi, various other staff members and therapists had witnessed the effects of Jordan's parents' neglect, which inevitably led to his deterioration. They also made several calls to the Oswego County Child Protective Services.

Jordan was allocated a physical therapist from Pemberton Associates. When he moved into the Mexico Central School District in September 2018, and she began working with him, a meeting with a special education committee was convened to set up a care plan for Jordan, which she and his parents attended. This vital component of Jordan's health and well-being covered both Jordan's at-home-care and his parents' expectations of his care during school hours.

The caring woman, who was an integral part of the team who wanted the best for him, told the committee that Jordan had outgrown his wheelchair, and it no longer "supported his physical needs". As a teenager, there was no need for Jordan to be pushed around by others, and a power chair with a joystick would have afforded him independence. With features that would have allowed him to stretch and move his body, it would have been life-changing for his health and well-being.

Without a visit to a doctor to write a prescription for a new wheelchair however, Jordan remained stuck in his old one, which along with being far too small, had fallen into disrepair. Lisa Waldron put off this visit many times, finally taking her son to a doctor in August 2020, where a prescription was obtained.

However, Waldron again delayed getting support for her son, and cancelled several appointments with the vendors of the much-needed wheelchair, until, six months after she received the doctor's prescription, she attended with Jordan. What could have been a lifeline for the 17-year-old, was denied him for almost three years, and he died just three months after it was finally obtained. I have not been able to ascertain whether Jordan was ever able to use it.

A caring occupational therapist, also from Pemberton Associates, worked with Jordan to help him reach his goals. The determined young man's desire for independence included a yearning to feed himself. In their twice weekly sessions during school term time, she and Jordan worked together for almost three years, with the teen making good progress at the beginning, learning to bring the spoon to his mouth without help. But following the 2019 spring break, the therapist witnessed a steady decline in her young charge's abilities. In addition, his worsening scoliosis made it more difficult for him to sit up straight, and with his head tilting further to the side, it was hard for him to eat. Kathi Davies also assisted in feeding Jordan, but despite his good appetite, and the food being cut into small pieces to help him swallow, he quickly became tired.

During virtual sessions, the occupational therapist found that Jordan would cry out in pain, and that he often had spasms in his legs. These point again to the teenager being left for lengthy periods without being helped to move his limbs.

Staff expressed their concerns to his mother, that Jordan was at risk of choking, with the potential for food to enter the airway, causing it to travel to the lungs. To decrease the likelihood of this happening, they recommended that he should be taken for a swallow test, with a view to acquiring a feeding tube. This could also have ensured that Jordan would consume enough calories to support his health, as the professionals felt that he was at great risk of becoming undernourished, due to the small amount he was eating. How right they were.

Lisa Waldron, however, claimed that Jordan was "eating just fine" and didn't take her son for this vital test.

§

Jordan's cause of death was sepsis and malnutrition. Weighing as little as a child half his age, Jordan was a mere 55 pounds when he died, and had open, bleeding sores.

We throw out terms like sepsis with abandon. This life-threatening condition occurs when the body cannot fight infection and the immune system overreacts, causing damage to the body's organs, principally the kidneys and the liver. In the words of Dr Derek Angus, a critical care physician at the University of Pittsburgh School of Medicine: "With sepsis, the fight between the infection and the body's immune response makes the body like a battleground. In the case of severe sepsis, that fight results in vital organ dysfunction, which puts one's life in peril."

The UK NHS and NHS Scotland websites clearly state that one way to prevent this condition is to clean and care for wounds. Symptoms of sepsis may include: a high temperature (fever) or low body temperature, chills and shivering, a racing heartbeat, fast breathing and confusion. When these symptoms cannot be controlled by the body's immune system, and without early treatment, the blood pressure can drop suddenly, leaving organs starved of oxygen, and septic shock ensues.

If left untreated, this will lead inevitably to a frightening and painful death. To know that Jordan could so easily have been spared this suffering, by simply moving him in his wheelchair, and cleaning any wounds that did occur, feels absolutely heart-breaking.

Although Jordan had died on May 9, 2021, his mother Lisa Waldron, 43, and stepfather Anthony Waldron, 37, were not charged, with manslaughter and criminally negligent homicide, until March 16, 2022. The charges were later upgraded to second-degree murder and first-degree assault.

Eighteen months later, in September 2023, Lisa Waldron pled guilty to manslaughter and assault, thereby avoiding trial, for which she was sentenced to 20 years in state prison.

In the period after the homicide, up to the day she was charged, Lisa Waldron had brazenly continued to receive her deceased son's disability benefits. It has been reported that she spent at least part of the money on fast food and trips to the beach. The court ordered her to pay restitution and that she should be on probation for the theft (of government property) for three years following her expected release from prison.

This indicates to me that, not only did Lisa Waldron have very little affection for her son, but she must also have felt confident that she would not be charged with any crime. Allowing him to wither and die on her watch, and then to gain financially after his death, seems callous in the extreme.

Anthony Waldron stood trial in Pulaski in October 2023 for his part in the crimes against his stepson. He was defended by his lawyer Salvatore Lanza, and prosecuted by Caleb Petzoldt, assistant district attorney, and Courtney Venditte, senior assistant district attorney.

Just one witness for the defence was called to the stand; the plaintiff's wife and co-accused, Lisa Waldron. Driven in handcuffs from prison and brought into the courtroom, she was questioned by both legal teams. Lisa Waldron described Anthony Waldron as having been a "helpful stepfather" up until he was injured in a serious car crash, after which he was unable to continue to share the caretaking role. It appears that she was admitting that she was the one to blame, and as she was already serving her sentence, perhaps hoped that her husband would be exonerated. However, on cross examination, Lisa was asked to provide details of what Anthony was and was not able to do, but did not adequately respond. Lisa's efforts did not affect the outcome for her husband.

The prosecution called several witnesses. Both Jordan's physical therapist and occupational therapist described a virtual meeting with Anthony and Lisa Waldron, with Jordan's team of special education therapists and teachers, along with the Committee of Special Education, that took place in March 2021. Claiming that they took good care of Jordan, Anthony Waldron, who had done most of the talking at the meeting, was upset and aggressive, complaining that following a call to child protective services, the school district was now harassing them. Support services were offered to the family on this, and multiple other, occasions, but the Waldrons' reluctance to take up the assistance left Jordan in a state of perpetual suffering.

Prosecutors made it clear that neglecting to obtain two simple things for Jordan, a swallow test, and an appropriate wheelchair, caused him unnecessary distress during the three years before he died.

Photographic exhibits at the trial showed a kitchen overflowing with food, lending further poignancy to Jordan's death being partly due to malnutrition.

Anthony Waldron made a number of outbursts in the courtroom. At one point, he slammed his hand on the desk and yelled during a witness' testimony: "Everyone keeps saying 'Lisa, Lisa, not me!'" presumably to demonstrate his innocence. Ordering the jury out of his courtroom, Judge Armen J Nazarian reprimanded Waldron, telling him to allow his representative to speak for him. Having warned the prisoner that any further commotion would revoke his bail conditions, the jury were called back in, and were advised to disregard

Waldron's conduct, as it was not evidence and "should not be considered in any way".

Anthony Waldron was found guilty and sentenced to 29 years to life for his part in Jordan's murder.

NOTE: The handling of reports of neglect, made by Jordan's teachers at Mexico High School, by Oswego Department of Social Services, was also called into question. Following an investigation, the department agreed that whilst they had always followed up on certain issues, they could only work with the information they had been given. The commission found that staff shortages led to the shortcomings encountered.

§

A candlelight vigil for Jordan was held at his high school on 26 March 2022.

With a small Facebook Group in his memory, it is good to know that this young man has not been forgotten, and perhaps if people read my books, and watch podcasts that raise awareness of these crimes, far into the future, he never will be.

MY NAME IS CHILD B

JESSICA JACKSON

Abuse of Children with Disabilities

Jordan is so clear in my mind as a quick-witted, intelligent young man, that for a long time, it didn't occur to me to explore the abuse of children with disabilities.

Along with babies under one year old, children with disabilities make up the highest proportion of children who are abused, whether they survive, or are abused to death.

Several children I have written about were, or became, disabled. In Volume 1 of my series, I tell the story of JaQuinn Brewton, a little boy with learning difficulties, which only made him more loveable in his siblings' eyes, but more easy to punish and terrorise in the eyes of his tormentors. In the same volume, the abuse of Michael Dickinson, whose mother had Munchausen's Syndrome by Proxy, rendered him physically disabled, being needlessly dependent upon the use of a wheelchair, unable to feed himself, etc.

Cerebral palsy (CP) covers a wide range of abilities. As recently as last night, I watched the UK Final of my not-so-secret TV addiction, The Traitors. Only when the series was almost finished did one of the winners reveal that he has CP. I had no clue, as his disability was largely invisible. And in my personal life, I have been very close to two people with the same disability as Jordan, but whose lives could hardly have been more different from his.

At University, on my first day of a sociology course, I met a young man with whom I remained friends throughout our time there, with more laughter and going to rock concerts than studying; although we also did a little of that too. We had many hilarious (for him) and exhausting (for me) nights pushing an extremely heavy electric wheelchair that had run out of juice up the hills of the Yorkshire city where we studied. He was one of the cleverest guys I've known, with an opinion on everything, especially Politics. Although we later lost touch, I remember seeing him on national television a few years later, presenting a current affairs program.

One of my dearest friends today was also born with cerebral palsy. But instead of having the misfortune to be born to neglectful parents, Jackie's mum and dad adored her, and afforded whatever support was needed to enable her to take on the challenges of her disability and overcome them with style. (NB: she's the most stylish woman I know!) To give her a good education, her parents moved the family from the town their forebears had lived in for generations to the opposite side of the country, moving back home when she completed her time at school. In her twenties, Jackie met and married a wonderful man and they ran a small business together for a number of years. She also served as a director for a local charity. When tragedy struck, and her husband suffered a sudden, massive brain haemorrhage at work, she was widowed at the age of 40. As I write this, 17 years after his death, I'm acutely aware that at this time in her life, my friend and her husband would have been continuing to enjoy their love of travel; an interest they had discovered they shared from the moment they met. Although her disability does affect her physically, my friend continues to live independently.

By contrast, Jordan's life, particularly the latter years, was made miserable by those who should have showered him with love and opportunities, and helped him to fulfil his undoubted potential.

A usable wheelchair can be a lifeline to someone whose physical disability affects their mobility. And with continuing technological advances, this piece of equipment can be tailored to meet the user's specific needs. Whilst the professionals involved with Jordan worked to put this in place, the lax attitude of his parents repeatedly put obstacles in their way.

Receiving nutrition via a feeding tube is not an ideal state of affairs for anyone. But for someone whose ability to swallow has become seriously impaired, it may be the best course of action. Once again, Jordan was prevented from receiving this life-changing intervention by his parents' unwillingness to act on his behalf and take him to the necessary medical appointments, one of which would have been a swallow test. Having said that, feeding tubes require scrupulous cleaning to keep them free from bacteria, and therefore whilst Jordan was not attending school, it is hard to imagine that the Waldrons would have maintained the standard of hygiene needed to keep him safe.

Whilst parenting a child with special needs is by no means easy, most parents meet the challenges with love and a willingness to make the necessary adaptations that will benefit all the family members. In some countries, there is little support for such families, and they must struggle on in isolation, but in Jordan's case, there were so many people ready to assist in keeping him free from pain, and encouraging his skills, that it is tragic that those closest to him refused to take advantage of the things that would have benefitted not only Jordan, but in many ways, would surely have made life easier for themselves.

Jordan is one of the 6-7 million children in the US who are victims of alleged abuse or neglect every year, and one of around 1,800 children whose torture ends in murder.

> That's 5 children, in the US alone,
> suffering and dying like Jordan, every day.

Jordan will never be forgotten by those who loved him, including caring family members, teachers and friends. And like other children who are abused to death, many of us who never knew him, hold him in our hearts and remember him in our own way. My way is by writing his story, in the hope that you will read and think of the fun-loving and stoical teenager, who never got the chance to grow into the wonderful man he could have been.

His name is Jordan Brooks

Please don't forget him

MY NAME IS CHILD B

Help Me To Raise Awareness

Children like Jordan are often neglected in death as well as life. So if you are able to spare a moment to rate or review his story, I'd be very grateful. Please do so in your usual way, or use the QR code or link to get back to the book's page:

https://mybook.to/Child-B

Then scroll waaay down
until you see Write a Review
(usually on the left side)

> Your review or rating will help to spread awareness of abuse, and just a star rating or a few words is enough.

Your Next Book In The Series

Coming Summer 2025

"I did legally punish my daughter."

These words spoken by Sara Sharif's father emphasise that in some cases, physically disciplining children can lead to murder.

After murdering her, Sara's father, stepmother, and uncle fled the country, later returning to face judge and jury for their crimes.

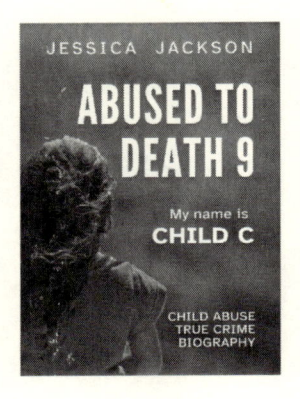

JESSICA JACKSON

ABUSED TO DEATH 9

My name is
CHILD C

CHILD ABUSE
TRUE CRIME
BIOGRAPHY

Find out as soon as it's published ...

Follow me on Amazon

And be the first to know when new books are released – the button to click is right beside my photo!

Use the QR code or link:

https://author.to/jessicajackson

*(Make sure your Settings in **Communications Preferences in your Amazon account** are set to receive info about new releases.)*

Join Us On Facebook

After Facebook, without explanation, **suspended my Page** to honour the murdered children, I lost all Followers, comments, and discussions.

All gone.

So please Follow Me as we start again!

Use the QR code or link:

Jessica Jackson Writer

Or within Facebook, type into the search bar:

Jessica Jackson Writer

Don't Miss A Thing

Pick up your free ebook:

Just scan this code:

https://BookHip.com/KXACJDT

Follow me on Facebook:
Jessica Jackson Writer

Follow me on Amazon:
https://author.to/jessicajackson

*(Ensure your Settings in **Communications / Preferences** in **Amazon** are set to receive info about new releases.)*

Have You Read All My Books?

Find them in your usual way, or you can ...

Search Amazon for:

Abused To Death by Jessica Jackson

Or scan this code:

Or use this link:

https://viewbook.at/abused-series

I'd love you to **Follow** me on Amazon too!

Prevention

Abuse and murder occur for complex reasons, and prevention is an immense task. These are my own views on how we can move towards prevention of this horrendous crime, echoing those of the World Health Organisation (WHO).

1 - End physical discipline of children
2 - Regulate homeschooling effectively
3 - An outlet for caregivers' anger
4 - Listen to the children when they report abuse
5 - Improve communication between agencies
6 - Safe places for unwanted babies
7 - Educate the parents of the future:
- that a baby communicates by crying
- how to give love, safety and guidance
- about bladder & bowel habits of children

Warning Signs of Abuse

There are various factors that might suggest a child is being abused. This list has been compiled by the NSPCC, but is not exhaustive:
- unexplained changes in behaviour or personality
- becoming withdrawn or anxious
- becoming uncharacteristically aggressive
- lacking social skills and having few friends
- poor bonding or relationship with a parent
- knowledge of issues inappropriate for their age
- running away or going missing
- wearing clothes which cover their body

And I would add:

- marks and bruises on the body
- being secretive
- stealing (often food)
- weight loss
- inappropriate clothing
- poor hygiene / unkempt
- tiredness
- inability to concentrate
- being overly eager to please the adult
- the child *telling* you that they're being hurt (alarmingly, this is often ignored)
- a non-verbal child *showing* you that they're being hurt

- the adult removing the child from school after they have come under suspicion

And when faced with an adult who you suspect of abusing a child, don't unquestioningly accept what they say, but instead:

        A - Assume nothing

        B - Be vigilant

        C - Check everything

        D - Do something

Listen to the children and report what you see

To report child abuse in The USA & Canada

The National Child Abuse Hotline: 1-800-422-4453

If a child is in immediate danger, call 911

To report child abuse in The UK

Adults, call the NSPCC on 0808 800 5000

Children, call Childline on 0800 1111

Or if there is risk of imminent danger, ring 999

To report child abuse in Australia

The National Child Abuse Reportline: 131-478
Children, call: 1800-55-1800
If a child is in immediate danger, call 000

Selected Resources

New York State Office of Child and Family Services – ocfs.ny.gov

- *Child Fatality Report SY-21-020 – 9 November 2021*
- *Family Assessment Response – Another road to safety*

CNY Central News – Mary Kielar:

- *18 March 2022 – CPS showed 'hostility and annoyance' when teachers tried helping disabled teen who died*
- *27 October 2023 – Jordan Brooks was always happy, says former aide as first week of stepfather's trial ends*
- *10 November 2023 – A kitchen full of food, a filthy wheelchair*

Facebook Group

- *Justice for Jordan and Galaxy*

Disclaimer

My aim is to tell stories of murdered children with a combination of accuracy and readability, to heighten awareness of child torture and murder, and to explore ways of preventing further tragedies. I have relied on the factual information available to me during my research, and where I have added characters or dramatised events to better tell the child's story, I believe I have done so without significantly altering the important details. If anyone has further information about the children, particularly if you knew them and have anecdotes to share about their life, I would be delighted to hear from you. Likewise, whilst every attempt has been made to make contact with copyright holders, if I have unwittingly used any material when I was not at liberty to do so, please contact me so that this can be rectified at:

jessicajackson@jesstruecrime.com

Manufactured by Amazon.ca
Acheson, AB